SITTING UP AT NIGHT
AND
OTHER CHINESE POEMS

Sitting Up at Night
and
Other Chinese Poems

SELECTED & TRANSLATED BY
Lau Tak Cheuk

The Chinese University of Hong Kong

Library of Congress Catalog Card Number: 73-92414

Set by T.P. Graphic Arts in Monophoto Apollo 645.
Printed in Hong Kong by Wah Chi Printing Co.

Contents

1 **Li Po**
Sitting up at night
To Meng Ta-jung, a Taoist in the Wang Wu Mountain
At night in the Tung Lin Monastery in Lu Shan

4 **Tu Fu**
Poem
Spring at the riverside

5 **Huang-fu Jan**
On the departure of the Monk An

6 **Ch'ien Ch'i**
On the river

Yao Hsi
Meeting a friend in Ching K'ou and seeing him off to Lung Chou

7 **Wang Chien**
An allegory of time
A song to the one far away
Poem

9 Meng Chi'ao
Autumn thoughts
The wandering son
Feeling
Complaint
Frivolous people along the River Pa

11 Chang Chi
Song
Autumn

12 Wang Ya
A frontier song

Han Yu
Farewell to a monk

13 Liu Yü-hsi
The round fan
The autumn fan

14 Po Chü-I
Lying ill in the country
Forced drinking
Consoling the mind
Growing old
End of the year

17 Liu Tsung-yüan
On waking up
A summer day

18 Li Chün-yü
Sitting before the fire

Yüan Chen
Illness

19   Chia Tao
The swordsman

    Li Ho
An old song

20   Li Shang-yin
No title
No title
To a Taoist
The sun shoots

22   Weng Ting-yün
To a friend from a villa in the suburb of Hu

    Tuan Cheng-shih
Song

23   Yü Fen
Han Shih

24   Lu Kuei-meng
The carnation
Love of flowers

25   Tzu Lan
On the city wall

    Wei Chuang
Song

    Han Shan
Poem

26   Kuan Hsiu
The cemetery
Mooring the boat on the river

28 Emperor Chuang Tsung
Song

Chang Hsien
Song

29 Mei Yao-chen
The green plums

Shao Yung
Lingering in bed

30 Yen Chi-tao
Song

Wang Ling
On weeping

31 Su Shih
To Chien, the Taoist

32 Huang T'ing-chien
Walking from a nap in a monastery
The return

33 Ch'ao Ch'ung-chi
Song

34 Ch'en Shih-tao
A reply to Master T'ien
Poem

35 Li Chih-yi
Song

Chu Tun-ju
Song
Song
Song
Song

38 Chen Yü-i
The tenth month
The Han Shih Festival
Spring

40 Wang Ch'ien-ch'iu
Song

Yang Wan-li
Reading

41 Lu Yu
To Chen Lu-Shan
Song
Spring rain

43 Fan Ch'eng-ta
Sitting alone in the study
Late autumn
On reading history
A winter day

45 Hsin Ch'i-chi
Song
Song

46 Ch'en Fu-liang
In dream I heard someone recite a poem, and on walking, I completed it.

47 Hsieh Hsi-i
Song

Chou Ang
Poem

48 Tai Fu-ku
Poem
Song

49 Shih Su
Changing things

Ou-yang Fu
Poem

50 Fang Yüeh
Spring

Lin Ching-hsi
On waking

51 Tai Piao-yuan
Closing the bag

52 Hsieh Ao
Strange! Strange!
Song of the spring bed-room

53 Liu Hsien
Song

54 Chang Yü
Lying ill in the South Mountain

55 Chen Shan-min
Grass

Cheng Hsieh
Bamboo

56 Peng Yun-hung
Insignificant life

Wang Jen
Poem

57 Yüan Mei
A thought

58 Chao I
Poem
Poem

60 Kung Tzu-chen
Thoughts

Li Po (701–762)

Sitting Up at Night

The winter night is cold and dreary.
I sit long and quietly in the north hall.
The well water is frozen; the moon comes into the
room.
The thickened blue light of the golden lamp sees me
weep.
The golden lamp goes out;
My weeping goes on.
Let me hide my tears
And hear you sing.
Your song has music
And I have feeling.
When music meets feeling,
There will be harmony.
But if there is one disagreeable phrase,
Your ten thousand tunes shall vibrate in vain the
dust on the beams.

To Meng Ta-jung, A Taoist in the Wang Wu Mountain

In the old days, by the Eastern Sea,
On the Lao Mountain, I fed on purple clouds.
With my own eyes I saw old An Ch'i*
Eat a date as large as a melon.
In middle age I went to court,
Was not happy and returned home.
Now from my red face the spring sun has faded;
White hairs indicate the end of life.
Still I hope to succeed in making the golden potion
And with flying steps mount the cloud carriage.
I will follow you to the heavenly terrace
Where we will leisurely sweep fallen flowers for the
immortals.

*An Ch'i: name of a legendary immortal

At Night in the Tung Lin Monastery in Lu Shan

To seek the green-lotus edifice
Alone I leave the city.
The Tung Lin bell sounds clear in the frost;
The Tiger Stream gleams white under the moon.
A divine scent fills the air
And divine music is played continuously.
I sit motionless in meditation.
Ten thousand worlds enter a hair;
The true mind rests in vacuity;
Rising and sinking are broken for long kalpas.

Tu Fu (712–770)

Poem

The second moon is half gone and the third moon is
*   coming.*
How many more springs will the aging man meet?
Let's not think of the endless things outside the body,
But drink up the limited number of cups before death.

Spring at the Riverside

Dense flowers and wanton buds wrap the riverside.
With faltering steps, I fight shy of spring.
But as long as poetry and wine can be pressed into
*   service,*
The white-haired man does not need anyone's
*   attention.*

Huang Fu-jan (714–767)

On the Departure of the Monk An

You left home as a boy
For the love of the snow-mountain man.
On the long road you will travel a thousand li,
The lonely cloud your sole companion.
In the water you see the moon;
On the grass you do not grieve over spring.
During long days in the empty grove
To what things will your heart be near?

Ch'ien Ch'i (8th Century)
On the River

The tow-path along the river is narrow;
The sands crumble and the banks are uneven.
All know that the way is treacherous,
But when they load, who is content to load light?

Yau Hsi (8th Century)
Meeting a Friend in Ching-k'ou and Seeing Him off to Lung Chou

The cicadas buzz with urgency
At sunset on the autumn tree.
This alone brings unbearable sorrow,
And my friend is parting for Lung Chou.
Oh, meeting and parting
Are equal on the road of straying sheep.

Wang Chien (8th–9th Century)
An Allegory of Time

What is gone is like a worn-out curtain;
What is come is like a new dress.
But freshness does not last long;
When its colour fades, it will be abandoned.
Who would have known that the moving will be
    short-lived?
Who would have known that the young will be old?
In the trivial, before-death hours,
We face each other with questions of right and wrong.
What was good to hear brings no pleasure;
What was good to look at suddenly develops flaws
One must understand that the nature of all things
Depends on the mood of the human heart.
In all time it has been like this.
What can the sages do?

A Song to The One Far Away

My love is gone I know not where.
She may be with the Wu Mountain moonlight or the
   Hsiang River rain.
We had a thousand meetings, but nothing was clear—
Stars at the bottom of the well, words in a dream.
Face to face, I found it difficult to know your heart.
Now that you are ten thousand li *away, I am full of*
   doubts.

Poem

On the tree, under the tree, I look for fallen petals;
Some have flown west and some east.
This comes of the peach flower's desire to bear fruit;
It's unfair to blame the nocturnal wind.

Meng Chiao (751–814)
Autumn Thoughts

Lonely bones at night lie with difficulty;
Singing insects call to me.
No tears come from an old man's sob
Autumn dew-drops fall for me.
The departure of youth was as sudden as scissor-
    snapped;
Coming infirmity will be as many-threaded as
loom-woven.
What touches the heart calls up no new impression;
In the cluster of grief are remnants of memory.
Have I the heart to follow the south-bound sail
In rivers and mountains to trend on former trails?

The Wandering Son

The thread in the good mother's hand
Makes clothing for the wandering son's back.
Before he goes, she stitches and stitches,
Fearing that he might delay and delay his return.
Who says the gratitude of the inch-long grass
Can repay the warmth of the spring sun?

9

Feeling

When I look at the muddy water, my heart is calm.
When I look at the clear stream, my desire is roused.
I wish to meet the man under the sea
And ask him for the moon inside the oyster.
Before this desire is satisfied,
My heart will know no peace.

Complaint

Let's test our tears, yours and mine.
We'll drop them into two different places in the pond
And see for whose tears
The lotus flowers of this year will die.

Frivolous People along the River Pa

In Ch'ang-an there is no loitering,
Especially in the evening twilight.
Meeting between the River Pa and the River Ch'an,
Even relatives do not stop for a sign of greeting.
I pity myself, a clumsy person,
Following the frivolous set;
Some day I may fail to step aside in time
And be turned into dust in the ruts.
Here too white hairs grow:
They have not ceased for the sake of fast running.

Chang Chi (8th–9th Century)
Song

In the garden the spring birds are pecking at the
*   branches;*
The red silk tunic is not yet finished.
To-day is the Earth God Festival; she puts down
*   thread and needle,*
Gets up and walks under the red cherry tree.

Autumn

In Lo-yang City the autumn wind blows again.
In my letter home I have so much to say.
Fearing I've left out something in my hurry,
I re-open it when the messenger is about to depart.

Wang Ya (8th–9th Century)
A Frontier Song

The young man leaves home and follows the general
With a precious sword and gold-bedecked saddle to
*   seek success.*
He knows not that the horse's bones are hurt by the
*   cold water;*
He only sees the evening clouds rise over the Dragon
*   City.*

Han Yü (768–824)
Farewell to a Monk

The monk loves the mountain and never goes out;
The layman tied to the world cannot promise future
*   visits.*
At the foot of the Chu Jung Peak I look back:
I know we will not meet again.

Liu Yü-hsi (772–842)
The Round Fan

I, the round fan, the round fan,
Served you in the summer palace.
But since the autumn wind entered the garden tree,
We have never met again.
The lady riding the phoenix
Is darkly covered with spider's web.
Next year inside your bosom
Will be fresh silk from the loom.

The Autumn Fan

Do not say that love returns not;
In the world honour and disgrace mutually jostle.
At the time I entered your bosom,
How could I have known that in the cold hearth
*   there were dead ashes?*

Po Chü-yi (772–846)

Lying Ill in the Country

Sadly embracing a serious illness,
I pass the dreary mornings and evenings.
No sooner do summer trees gather shade
Than autumn herbs sparkle with dew.
The nest eggs of last week
Now fly away as young birds.
The caterpillars of yesterday
Cast off their skin and turn into cicadas.
The four seasons roll on
And not one thing can stay put.
Only in the sick man's heart
Does a sinking feeling persist.

Forced Drinking

If one sits not in Buddhist meditation to melt absurd
  desires,
One must get drunk and sing mad songs;
Otherwise in nights of autumn moon and spring wind,
How can one prevent the past from coming back into
  the idle mind?

Consoling the Mind

The dark hair grows daily whiter;
The white face grows daily darker.
In life before death
Changes are endless.
Of what we call our possessions,
What can be nearer than our features and complexion?
When changes come
Nothing can stop them.
Far less can we control things outside the body—
The smooth road or the blocked path.

Growing Old

To-day and then to-morrow,
And old age steals upon us.
White hairs come off with the comb;
The rosy face says good-bye to the mirror.
One feels lonely in spring;
Little joy comes from wine;
Sorrow and bitterness accompany most events;
The faces one sees are seldom those of old friends.
I know my bodily clay is part of the universe,
Which incessantly turns.
What puzzles me is the disappearance of the youthful
* heart;*
Where can that have spent itself?

End of the Year

In a half-worn green gown, with a half-white head,
Against the frosty wind I climb the riverside tower.
I must have unconsciously made progress in Ch'an
* Buddhism;*
It's time I felt sad, but I don't.

Liu Tsung-yüan (773–819)
On Waking Up

I wake up and through the empty window
The desolate rainy sky dawns.
Pleasure excursions are sadly retarded;
Trivial affairs are unexpectedly many and distracting.
I make inquiries into ways of dealing with the world;
The ancients have not exhausted them.

A Summer Day

In the southern town, intense heat intoxicates like
   wine.
With the north window open, I lean on the table and
   have a nap.
When I wake up at noon, all is silent:
Only the village boy is grinding tea outside the hedge.

Li Ch'ün-yü (8th–9th Century)
Sitting Before The Fire

The lonely lamp shines on the sleepless man;
Wind and rain fill the western woods.
So many things come into the mind:
I write in the ashes till late at night.

Yüan Chen (779–831)
Illness

My heart is like ashes and my hair like silk.
Even if I were hale and strong, what would be the
  use?
The family is provided for and I am free;
It's time to lie ill at leisure.

Chia Tao (779–843)
The Swordsman

For ten years I have been sharpening a sword;
Its frosty blade has not yet been tried.
Now I show it to you:
Who is complaining of injustice?

Li Ho (790–816)
An Old Song

The white shadow goes home on the western mountain.
Infinitely high is the blue.
Where do past and present end?
A thousand years float in the wind.
The sea sand turns into stone;
Fish blow foam on the Ch'in Bridge;
Space and light extend far into the distance;
The bronze pillar thins year by year.

Li Shang-yin (813–858)
No Title

Where is the mournful tseng* *accompanying the*
urgent pipe?
In the cherry lane along the willow bank.
The old maid of the east house cannot marry herself
off.
In mid-April, when the sun is bright in the sky,
On a warm day after Ch'ing Ming,# she watches by
the wall
The fourteen-year old Princess of Li Yang.
She goes home and tosses in bed till dawn;
The swallows on the beam can hear her long-drawn
sighs.

**Tseng: a stringed instrument.*
#*Ch'ing Ming: a festival in the third month of the*
lunar year.

No Title

When she was eight, she secretly looked into the mirror
And was able to paint long eye-brows.
When she was ten, she went on promenades
And wore a skirt with lotus flowers.
When she was twelve, she learned to play the tseng
And never put down the silver nail-piece.
When she was fourteen, she lived among relatives
And was yet unmarried.
Now she is fifteen; she weeps in the east wind
And averts her face under the swing.

To a Taoist

We went up the clouded mountains together but you
  stayed behind.
On the Yang Tai Peak, the white path is as narrow as
  a thread.
You must be leaning against the three-pearl tree
Forgetting it's now in the world the time of falling
  leaves.

The Sun Shoots

The sun shoots through the window and the wind
  shakes the door.
I wipe my hands on a scented silk; spring's desire is
  frustrated.
The winding corridors on four sides shut in solitude;
The green parrot looks on the red roses.

Wen Ting-yün (9th Century)
To a Friend from a Villa in the Suburb of Hu

Cupping my cheeks I look at the smooth green;
Ten thousand things converge upon my mind.
By the south pond after rain,
All the grasses look lush and fresh.
The quiet bird knows me not;
The fair lady cannot be expected to come.
Vainly abandoned to wanton movements
Is the melancholy spring time.

Tuan Cheng-shih (9th Century)
Song

Leisure is good.
Dusty affairs entangle not the mind.
I sit facing the tree before the window
And watch its shade move in three directions.

Yü Fen (9th Century)
Han Shih*

In April by the countryside,
Even common flowers are sweet.
A girl in white weeps at a new grave.
The wood-cutter's axe sounds among the tender
*   branches.*
A farmer takes his yellow dog
And hunts the fox on a hill.
In front of a grave he calls his dog;
He is not aware his head is as white as snow.

*Han Shih: a festival in the third month of the lunar
*   year.*

Lu Kuei-meng (9th Century)

The Carnation

I saunter along the river unheeded,
A drunken man living in the clouds for ten years.
Obligingly I untie the knot in the carnation
And release the reckless spring on the branches.

Love of Flowers

The human life span is one hundred years;
That of flowers is one spring.
When wind and rain come,
They will turn into dust in one day.
If flowers could feel sad,
They would be sadder than we who gaze at them.

24

Tzu Lan (9th Century)
On the City Wall

Old graves are thicker than grasses;
New graves encroach on the highway.
Outside the city, all the ground is occupied;
Inside the city men are still growing old.

Wei Chuang (836–910)
Song

I shall take a walk on a spring day,
When the wind blows apricot flowers on one's head.
If in the park I meet a gallant enough young man,
I will marry him without hesitation.
He might prove faithless and forsake me,
But I would not regret it.

Han Shan (9th–10th Century)
Poem

On my body a space-flower suit;
On my feet a pair of tortoise-hair shoes;
I hold a hare-horn bow
And try to shoot the dim-witted demon.

Kuan Hsiu (9th–10th Century)

The Cemetery

The rabbit* does not delay;
The crow# makes haste.
The Emperor Mu© whipping his eight horses
Is not fast enough for them.
Therefore in the cemetery
Graves come up apace.
The once head-in-the-clouds,
Dragon-leaping, phoenix-perching,
Are all wind-scattered, earth-eroded,
Fox-gnawed, ant-picked.
The yellow gold does not weep;
The white jade does not sob.
Aspens rustle
In howling wind and gloomy moon.
Among broken tombstones and statues,
Weed-soiled and thorn-buried,
Cattle and sheep shuffle,
And shepherd boys play with withered bones.

*Rabbit: symbol for the moon.
#Crow: symbol for the sun.
©Emperor Mu (947–928 B.C.): legend says he had
  eight fast horses.

Mooring the Boat on the River

The banks look like Tung T'ing* and the mountains
*   like Shan.*[#]
The boat floating on the clear stream is cooler than a
*   bamboo mattress.*
The moon is bright; the wind is high; I cannot sleep;
Among the dry reeds, a fisherman is crying out in a
nightmare.

*Tung T'ing: a lake in Hunan Province.
[#] Shan: a district in Chekiang Province.

Emperor Chuang Tsung (reigned 923–925)

Song

One leaf falls!
I raise the bead screen;
The scene is desolate.
On the painted hall the moon throws her cold
    shadow;
The west wind moves the silk curtains.
The silk curtains rustle
And old memories come to mind.

Chang Hsien (990–1078)

Song

Shyly smoothing her black locks,
She throws me happy glances.
The thirteen strings on the carved pegs
All sing like spring orioles.
Lovely clouds are soon scattered,
And broken dreams nowhere to be found.
The wide courtyard shuts in the evening twilight;
Showers of rain beat on banana leaves.

Mei Yao-ch'en (1002–1060)

The Green Plums

The plum leaves cannot yet hide birds,
But the green plums can be picked.
A girl from a small house south of the river
Plays with them outside the door.
Their sour taste sets her teeth on edge
And she throws them away without hesitation.
She pays no heed to the young men on horseback;
In spring the highway is full of them.

Shao Yung (1011–1077)

Lingering in Bed

Half-remembered and half-forgotten, the dream
    after waking;
Half-saddening and half-pleasing, the weary feeling;
I cling to my sheets, lie on my side and delay
    getting up.
Outside the screen falling flowers fly in profusion.

Yen Chi-tao (11th Century)
Song

My heart grieves that the flower season is ending.
After our parting, your image is always in my eyes.
The scented sheet still smells of your perfume;
Every time I return from my dream, I am full of
    tears.
You may not believe my heart is broken.
Who will bring me warmth in these cold nights?
I wish to make a love-contract with you for the next
    life;
Only I fear that it might again be short-lived.

Wang Ling (1032–1059)
On Weeping

Though the eye is where tears come from,
The heart is the original source.
The white sun shines on my face
As if to dry the falling drops.
But as it shines not into my heart,
How are my tears to become dry?
Moreover, thick clouds now cover the sun;
Where shall I find peace?

Su Shih (1036–1101)
To Ch'ien, The Taoist

The scholar has too much faith in books;
Practical affairs are to him only guess-work.
Overestimating his own capacity,
He lightly gives momentous promises.
At the time he is pleased with himself,
But afterwards overwhelmed with shame.
What a world of iron
Must be cast into such a mistake!
I have had my share of sorrow and misfortune;
I am always afraid of falling into sin.
Quietly looking back, I am glad;
I am not too far advanced for retreat.
As for you, Master Ch'ien,
You never commit yourself to anything.
What advice can I give you?
No ailment, no medicine.

Huang T'ing-chien (1045–1105)

Waking from a Nap in a Monastery

The fire has gutted and the water has ebbed in my
*   sick body,*
A heap of dust in space waiting for distintegration.
Yet I will make an effort to gather some young
*   friends*
Pick flowers and enjoy the spring of our dreams.

The Return

I packed my bag and went abroad to seek truth,
And travelled all over the world.
Long wandering had its troubles;
My horses were hungry and my servants grew thin.
I come back to my hill.
Everything is as of old.
I prune the overgrown ears of corn
And prod the cattle and sheep that lag behind.
Leaning against the table, I find all is calm;
My six senses suddenly become keenly perceptive.

Ch'ao Ch'ung-chih (11th–12th Century)
Song

I remember on the west pond we used to drink
*   together,*
And for years we had much pleasure.
After our parting, you sent me not a single line.
Even if we happen to meet again,
Things will not be the same.
I will sleep soundly to-night behind the brocade
*   screen;*
When the moon is bright, it's time to cross rivers
*   and lakes.*
I will ask no more questions about your feeling.
I know well when spring is gone,
It can no longer concern itself with fallen flowers.

Ch'en Shih-tao (1053–1101)
A Reply to Master T'ien

What is there so good in wine
That people refuse to forget it?
If you have no sorrow to dissolve,
Why make intoxication your abode?
It remains with us to discuss strange words;
We can keep hidden our secret recipes.
Even if one has beautiful flesh and bone,
It is necessary to draw long eye-brows.

Poem

Pleasing books are too soon finished;
Good company cannot be often had.
Things in the world are so contrary;
How many times does the heart get satisfaction in a
*   hundred years?*

Li Chih-yi (11th–12th Century)
Song

Fame since olden days has been like a migratory-bird.
The sun and the moon have never avoided the
*   overturned tub.**
Leave right and wrong to the mosquitoes at our ears.
Chance meeting with wind and thunder may prove
*   useful.*
When you walk under eaves, stoop low.
In wine there is another universe.

*Overturned tub: an old proverb says, "The sun does
*   not shine under the overturned tub."*

Chu Tun-ju (11th–12th Century)
Song

The autumn wind again comes into the world
And leaves rustle.
I see an endless expanse of misty waves
But no green hills.
Business of our precarious life,
Water of the Long River,
When do they have a respite?
Luckily it has always been like this;
Let us smile.

Song

Old age is lovable.
I have experienced the human world,
And know well what exists beyond the tangible.
Having seen through emptiness,
I crush the sea of grief and mountain of sorrow.
Neither allured by flowers,
Nor confused by wine,
I am wide awake everywhere.
When I have eaten my fill, I seek sleep;
Waking from sleep, I play whatever games chance
*   brings.*
Do not talk to me of the past or the present;
In the old man's mind
There's no place for such things.
I do not pray to gods,
Or cringe before Buddhas,
Nor do I imitate the restless Confucius.
I am too lazy to strive with you people.
Laugh at me if you like;
Whatever is is.
I am about to finish my part in the comedy;
My motley I will pass on to some other fool.

Song

If one believes that in emptiness nothing exists,
What is there for discussion?
When the wind is high, the white cloud scuttles;
The wind minds not whether it moves or stops,
Neither does the cloud whether it appears or hides.
Do not listen to the idle words of the ancients;
In the end you miss the horse and the sheep.
Your own intestine and stomach you must examine
*   for yourself.*
When everything is broken,
A big halo will be released.

Song

The paper curtain and the silk sheet keep me very
*   warm;*
Freely I toss about in my bed.
When I awaken the lamp at the west window burns
*   low;*
It's just mid-night.
The remnants of dreams I dismiss from my mind.
The time to come will be short.
I will untie the harness and free myself from
*   bondage,*
And what is past cross out with one stroke of the
*   pen.*

Ch'en Yü-i (1090–1138)
The Tenth Month

The north wind of the tenth month hastens the year's
*   end;*
The dust of the nine highroads stains the scholar's hat.
The returning crow at sunset flies by instinct;
The old goose on the long cloud finds going difficult.
I wish to visit high officials but fear cold remarks.
I will get some turbid wine that brings pure pleasure.
I sit alone reciting poetry by the mid-night moon.
The bare tree has no branches to be affected by the
*   cold.*

The Han Shih Festival

Behind the bamboo hedge I pass the Han Shih Festival.
A drizzle dilutes the spring feeling.
Noise never suits me;
In solitude I find my taste.
On the empty mountain, flowers wave and tremble;
Among straggling rocks, water makes warp and woof.
I lean on my stick; the day is soon ended.
What actually does one expect of life?

Spring

In the morning, the birds sing on the garden trees;
Red and green announce spring in the woods.
Good poetry suddenly stares me in the eye;
But before I can arrange the words it has vanished.

Wang Ch'ien-ch'iu (12th Century)
Song

Heroes' portraits are hung in the imperial gallery,
While their bones are divided by ants.
Why not, when you are alive,
Drink to flowers and orioles?
Clouds and mountains are quiet and friendly;
Heaven and earth are infinitely wide.
Smooth out the wrinkles on your brow;
Nothing ever happens according to the heart's desire.

Yang Wan-li (1124–1206)
Reading

A friend came from a distant place
And gave me a book.
I am tired of old books,
But a new book excites my curiosity.
On first reading, I feared it might finish too soon,
But after a little, its beauty began to dim.
Knowing it would give me no further interest,
I still made an effort to read on,
Hoping that among the dregs
I might find a tasty morsel
At the end I found nothing;
My only reward was fatigue and dizziness.
Great fatigue produces sleep,
Which is better than insomnia.

Lu Yu (1125–1210)
To Ch'en Lu-shan

Among wealth and rank you know few faces;
Precious jewels sparkle in vain in your breast.
Now you raise your hand to shield the western sun;
There must be floating dust that stains your coat.
Of old learning I know the standard must not be
  lowered;
But holding on to it, where can we go?
Last night, listening to wind and rain in the empty
  hall,
I suddenly remembered your subtle words before the
  lamp.

Song

I do not have four eyes or two mouths,
But my long stay in the world has given me experience.
Life and death are the twinkling of an eye;
Success and failure are the turning of the palm.
A few pairs of shoes will wear away the days and
*   months*
And a cup of wine will mint the wisdom of the ages.
Unlike dead dogs and horses, I need no old curtain for
*   a shroud;*
I give no thought to rushes and willows withering in
*   wind and frost.*
A smokeless chimney has become a common sight in
*   my house.*
The tortoise, the cicada and me are three good friends.
I am sure my name will not go down in history,
Unless starvation should confer immortality on me.

Spring Rain

Hardly has the bright sun set from the west window,
When from the eaves I hear the sound of falling rain.
My anxious heart needs no tortoise* forecast;
When flower time is ruined, fine weather will set in.

*Tortoise: the tortoise shell was used for fortune-
*   telling.*

42

Fan Ch'eng-ta (1126–1193)

Sitting Alone in the Study

The noonday sun roasts open the nutmeg bud.
The fighting sparrows raise the dust on the eaves.
My dim, tired eyes, finding no place to rest themselves
    on,
Follow the incense smoke to the top of the bamboo tree.

Late Autumn

The market noise surges like battle drums;
The sun's shadow moves like a rising tide.
I melt vain desires by counting breaths in meditation
And studying light and shade behind tightly-closed
    doors.

On Reading History

The making and marring of a hundred years depend
  on machination;
But in the end one is food for the vulture or the ant.
I pick the wick of the oil lamp,
And with dim eyes mete out judgment on past cases.

A Winter Day

I use the resinous pine branch as a candle.
Its thick smoke, black as ink, darkens my room.
This morning I cleaned the paper of the south window;
Now the evening sun looks twice as red.

Hsin Ch'i-chi (1140–1207)
Song

For this life I've decided not to question Heaven.
Alone I lean on the high tower;
Alone I lean on the high tower
And don't believe there's sorrow in the world.
You happen to come at my sleeping time.
You had better go;
You had better go
And tell the west wind I don't mind autumn.

Song

Old and infirm, I feel the attack of months and years.
A happy moment is worth a thousand pieces of gold.
All my life I've owed no debt to streams and hills.
No medicine can cure my addiction to books.
Let them call me clever or clumsy;
To me floating and sinking are the same.
Men are different in face as in heart.
There's no harm in writing down the details of my life;
I want to add my biography to the laughing stocks.

Ch'en Fu-liang (1141–1207)

In A Dream I Heard Someone Recite Part of A Poem and on Waking, I Completed It

Three men share a quilt.
In the cold night, they start a tugging battle.
One man is ashamed of the discourtesy,
Rises, sits up and waits for the morning sun.
Would the morrow again bring rain and snow
And patience be unrewarded with spring charm?
The four seasons follow the natural cycle.
The two men are in snoring slumber.

Hsien Hsi-i (12th–13th Century)
Song

The two oars stir up gentle ripples;
Along the banks, the mountains run in chains.
You will go home and I shall go home.
Say, how are we going to live afterwards?
I will certainly not think of you;
You must not think of me.
Your heart, which hitherto I have had for keeping,
You can now give to another.

Chou Ang (12th–13th Century)
Poem

A cool shade never leaves the evergreen tree.
The good taste of tea lingers all day long.
The poetic spell unsuppressed takes root in the heart.
Worldly affinity beginning to end, the eye sees no
    flowers.

Tai Fu-ku (1167–?)

Poem

The yellow gold has insufficient colour;
The white jade has slight blemishes.
If in people you do not demand perfection,
I would like to grow old with you.

Song

The Old Man of Shih P'ing*
Regrets that he is not living in the mountain.
All his life he has been resigned to fate;
Now he is old, he gives no thought to the business of
*   the world.*
Dumbness is better than eloquence.
He is poor but happy,
And he makes good use of fair weather.
His only wish is to have a head to grow white hairs
*   upon;*
That yellow gold is nowhere to be found worries him
*   not;*
When there is wine, he pours himself some.

*The Old Man of Shih P'ing; the pen name of Tai
*   Fu-ku*

Shih Su (12th–13th Century)
Changing Things

In changing things one can forget oneself.
Heavenly space does not need the mind.
To the sweet meat smell ants gather;
On the quiet tree cicadas buzz.
The deep water of the ruined well tires the fetcher;
The weed-filled garden draws no neighbourly visitors.
I pillow my head on my book and take a rest;
In the twilight, half the wall is shadowed.

Ou-yang Fu (12th–13th Century)
Poem

The wet faded red petals linger on the tree;
The willow fluff clothes the pond.
Of late all my desires have turned into cold ashes;
I will let Spring go home without a word of farewell.

Fang Yüeh (1199–1262)
Spring

The spring wind is kept very busy.
It must attend to flowers and trees;
To help swallows get mud and bees gather honey,
It must blow in a drizzle and bring back sunshine.

Lin Ching-hsi (1242–1310)
On Waking

I wake up in a lonely inn; the moonlight fills the
  autumn air.
Somewhere the sound of beating clothes calls up
  sadness in my mind.
In the depth of night the lotus leaves stir without a
  breeze;
On the cold water there must be sleepless gulls.

Tai Piao-yuan (1244–1310)
Closing the Bag

Out of ten visitors nine understand not;
The one that understands happens to be my enemy.
It's like two cleverly drawn eye-brows
Looking into the same mirror: they shame each other.
I regret I have no wide circle of friends;
Lasting bonds are difficult to form.
I close my bag and excuse myself to the young men:
"What I hoard up is not what you require."

Hsien Ao (1249–1295)
Strange! Strange!

Strange! Strange!
Wild winds blow up clouds from the grassy mound;
Bamboo dust darkly screens the hill.
The cock flies up the tree and the hawk dives into the
*   sea.*
In the world old routine turns new heads white.
The small boy of Huai Nan knows no sorrow.
The old man of Huai Nan lacks the strength to shout;
He fills an earthenware with water and looks at the
*   sun's eclipse.*

Song of the Spring Bed Room

Her hand touches the faded red; her hair she is too
*   lazy to comb.*
A sweet scent follows the butterfly that alights on
*   her skirt.*
The warm wind blows in sleep; she says not a word,
Goes back to bed and reads the dream-book.

Liu Hsien (1268–1350)

Song

Weary with spring sleep,
I walk round the flowering branches.
Yesterday's new red has changed to-day;
I crush it fine and dye my sleeves.
Green fans in the wind wave in my face;
Sunny threads fly away and return.
The willow flowers outside the screen and the swallows
*   inside*
Meet and seem to ignore each other.

Chang Yü (1277–1348)
Lying Ill in the South Mountain

The divine dragon lives in the big abyss;
A cup of water fills the outer wall.
He hides himself in a place extremely remote,
Yet he communes with the oceans.
At the peak, he makes an inch of cloud,
And at the foot of the mountain torrents of rain.
"If the corn dries up, it's not my fault;
If it is well-watered, it's not my merit.
Between heaven and earth, there exists Cruelty.
Out of its breath who can escape?"

Chen Shan-min (13th Century)
Grass

When the grass withers, its roots do not die.
In spring it flourishes again.
Sorrow also has its roots,
But it sprouts without waiting for spring.

Cheng Hsieh (1693–1760)
Bamboo

Knots and knots;
A thousand branches and ten thousand leaves;
But I will not blossom
To lure bees and butterflies.

Peng Yün-hung (18th Century)
Insignificant Life

In dreams I stand between heaven and earth,
Unable to measure their height and depth.
Through the curtain I look at sun and moon,
Unable to tell fair weather from foul.
Between the curtain and the dream,
I live all my life in doubt.

Wang Jen (18th Century)
Poem

The morning sun shines into the room;
The spring air warms the flowers.
She looks eagerly into the mirror,
But it is not yet light enough.
For three years she has been embroidering two
*   phoenixes*
With full detail of gesture and expression.
Would she spare any effort with thread and needle
And make the bright feathers short?

Yüan Mei (1716–1795)
A Thought

I did not want this life;
Suddenly I was born into the world.

And death will suddenly come.
After death and before birth,
The taste must be the same.
Still I dislike the idea that to the universe
One superfluous event should be added.

Chao Yi (1727–1814)
Poem

Spring flowers, we find, are too many;
Autumn flowers, we find, are too few.
Why not take some spring flowers
To adorn old autumn?
But Heaven will not consent
To please men by fulfilling their wishes.
We must know once life is created,
Heaven's job is finished.
How stupid are the people of the world,
Who send to Heaven their many importunities!
When there is injustice, they complain of being
*   wronged;*
When they get something, they complain of
*   insufficiency.*
Heaven is tired of the noise;
So it sits high above the blue.

Poem

Every night I see the bright moon,
So I have come to know her very well.
I ask her if she knows me.
She says, "I don't remember you.
In this wide, wide world,
Living things number by their millions
When there are great heroes,
I may rub my eyes a little for them.
As for people like you,
Who have done nothing outstanding,
If I were to get to know everyone,
How could I have such eyesight?
When the divine dragon moves in the air,
Ants bow to him.
Courteous they may be,
But heeded they are not."

Kung Tzu-chen (1792–1841)

Thoughts

A subtle state of mind is difficult to arrest;
Its stay is only of short duration.
Language cannot fix meaning.
In immense space my thoughts float.
After the aroma of tea has penetrated me to the bone,
The shadow of flowers climbs on my lap.
In eternity the moon peeps over the western pavilion;
For whom is she so patiently waiting?